Special thanks to
Danilo Zejak and Makiko Nishizawa

First US edition 2022
First published by
Berbay Publishing (Australia) 2020

Library of Congress Catalog Card Number pending
ISBN 978-1-5362-2145-9

22 23 24 25 26 27 APS 10 9 8 7 6 5 4 3 2 1

Printed in Humen, Dongguan, China

This book was typeset in Futura.
The illustrations were done in cut paper.

Candlewick Studio
an imprint of
Candlewick Press
99 Dover Street
Somerville, Massachusetts 02144

www.candlewickstudio.com

Whose Bones Are Those?

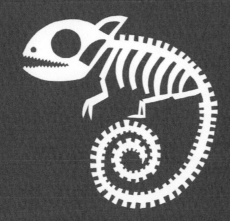

Chihiro Takeuchi

CANDLEWICK  STUDIO
an imprint of Candlewick Press

WHOSE BONES?

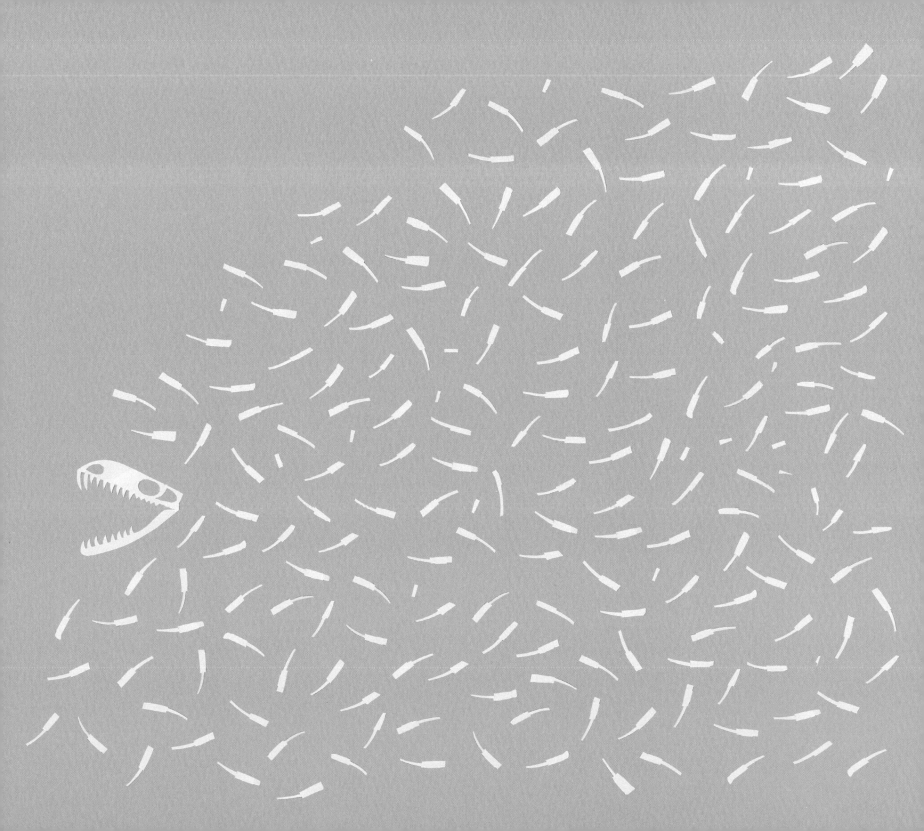

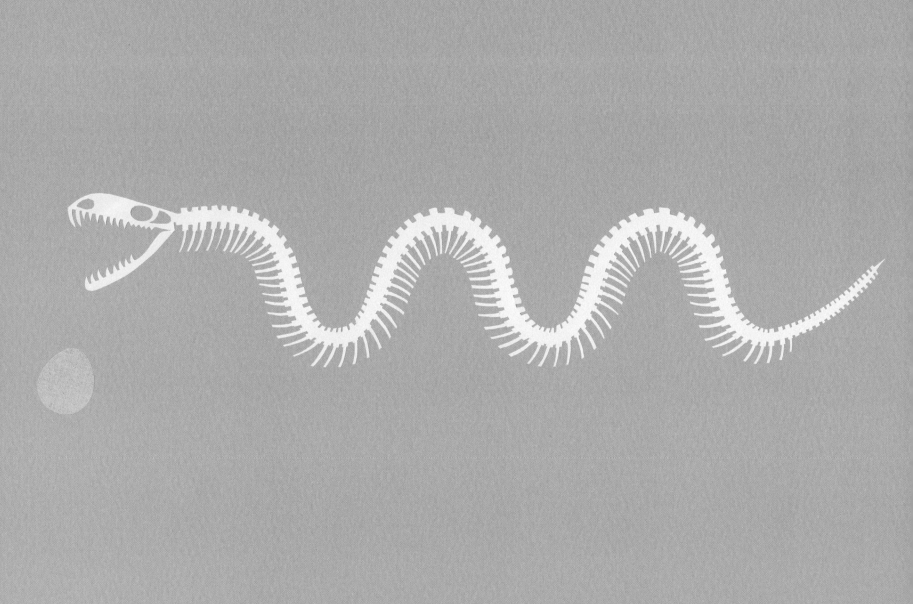

A snake!

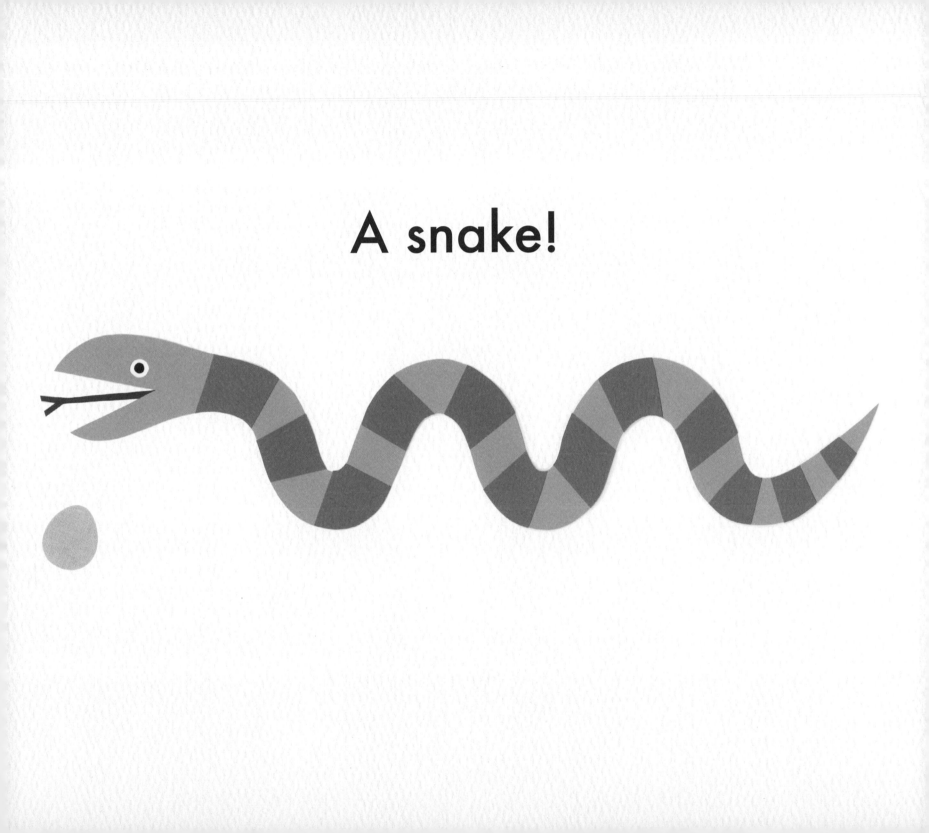

WHOSE BONES?

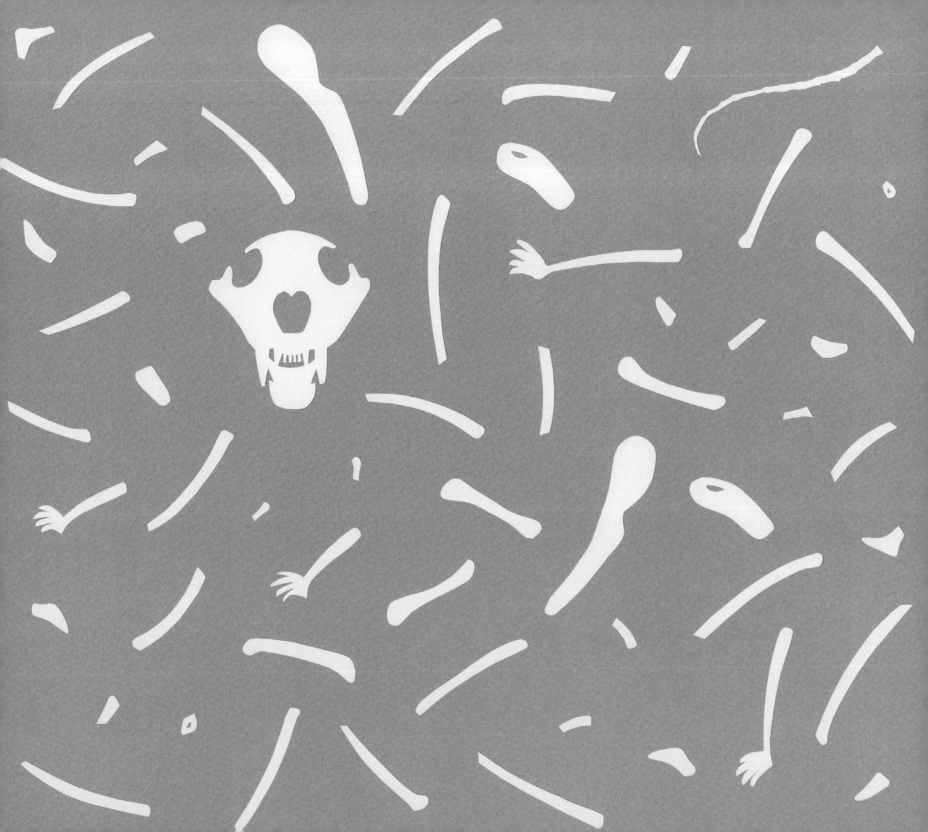

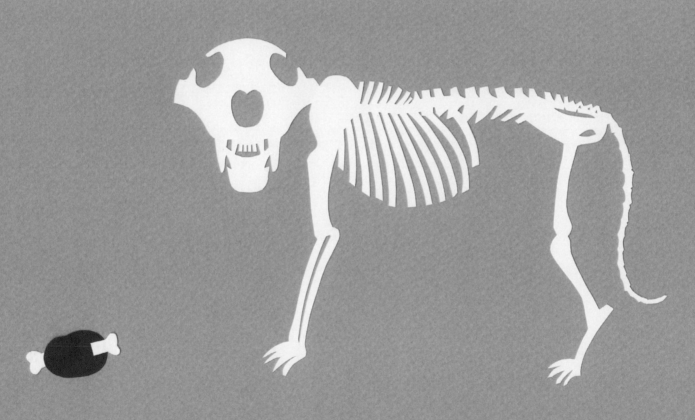

A lion!

WHOSE BONES?

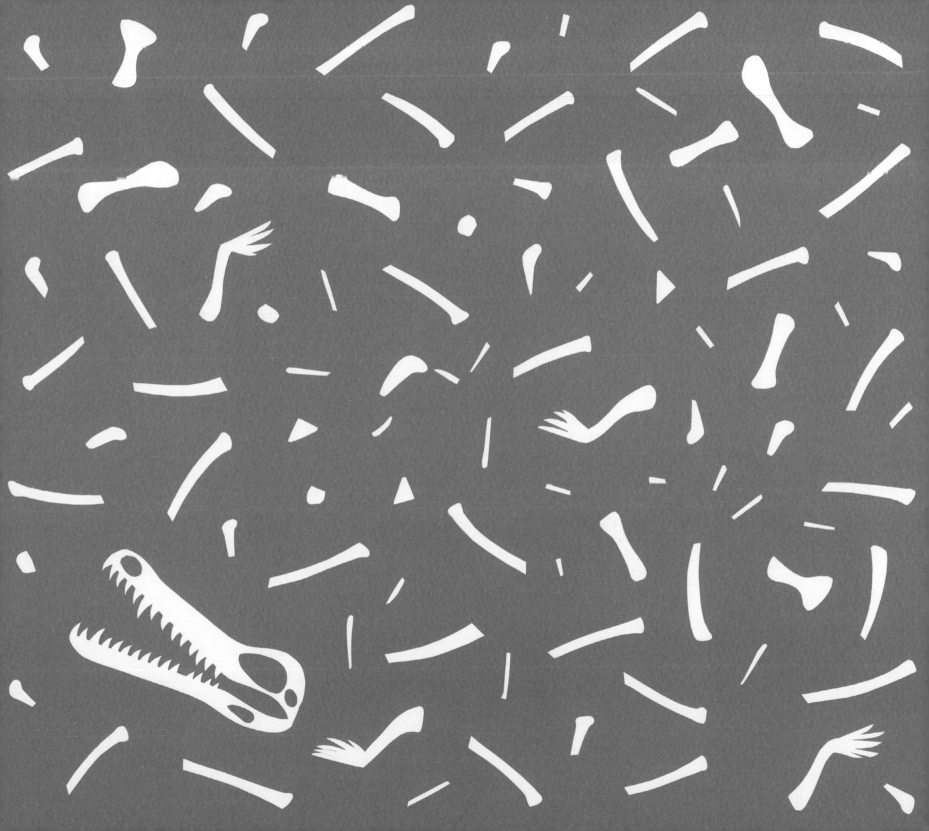

A crocodile!

WHOSE BONES?

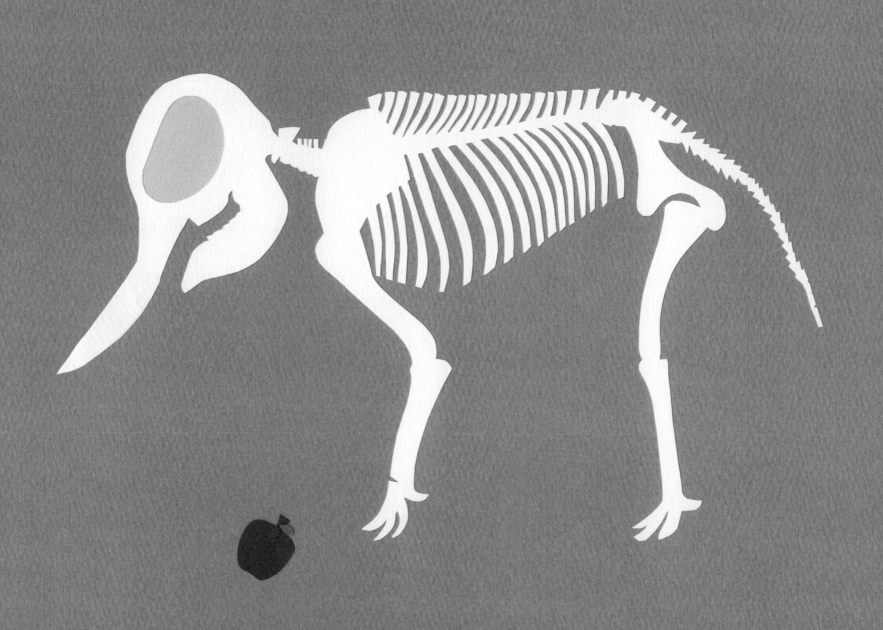

An elephant!

WHOSE BONES?

Flamingos!

WHOSE BONES?

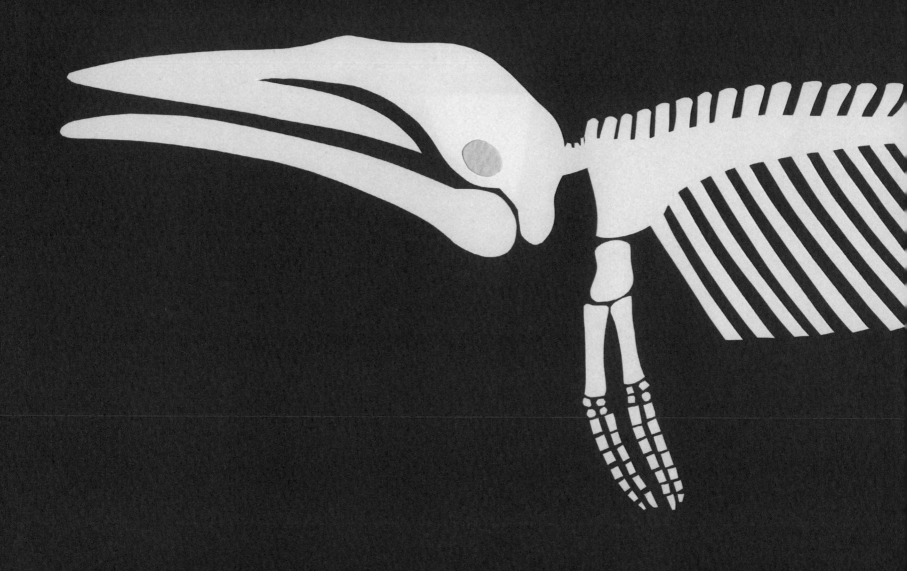

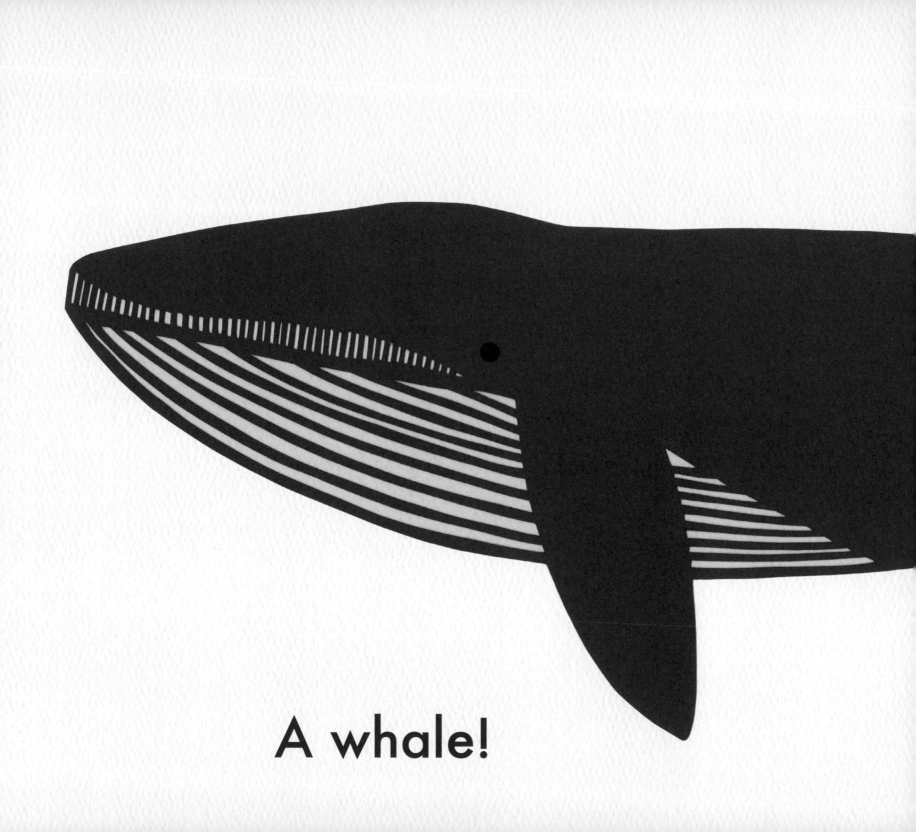

A whale!

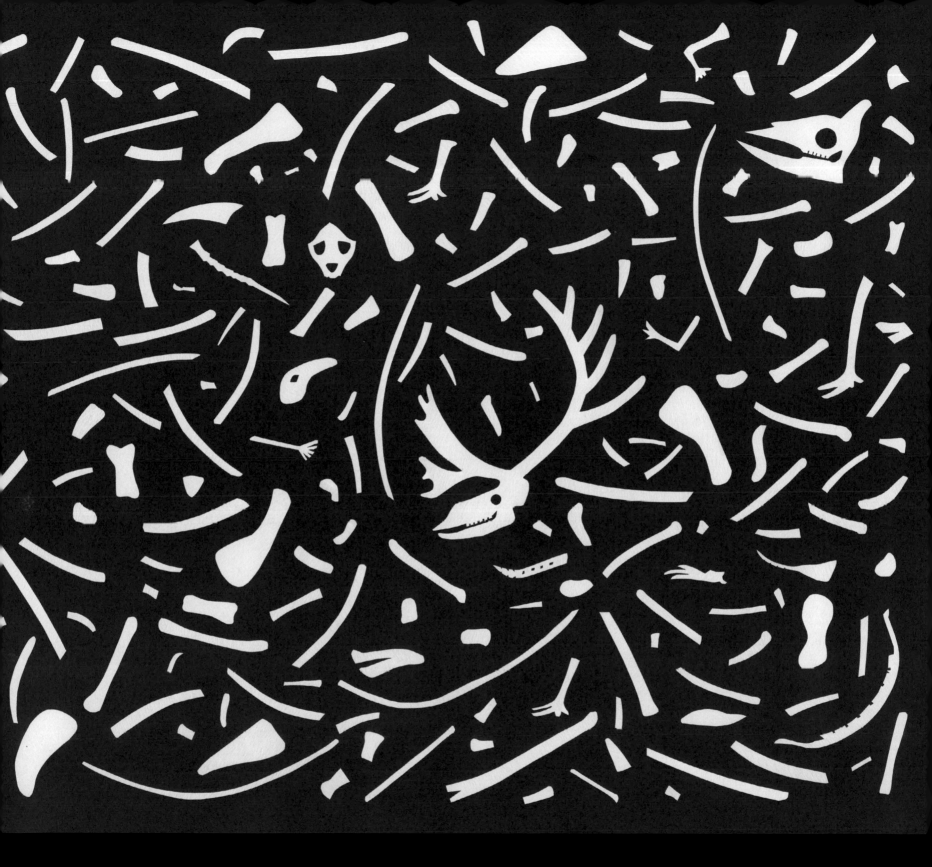

WHOSE BONES?

A bat!

A reindeer!

A penguin!

A turtle!

A rhinoceros!

A giraffe!

FUN FACTS

Did you know that all of the animals in this book are vertebrates?
That means they each have a backbone and skeleton.

 Did you know that a snake has no external
ears and more than four hundred bones?
That's a lot more bones than a human has.

 Did you know that male lions weigh around
400 lbs./181 kg on average but their bones only
weigh 20 lbs./9 kg? That's less than the average
skeleton of a human adult male or female.

 Did you know a crocodile is constantly
replacing its teeth? It can go through
thousands of teeth during its lifetime.

 Did you know that an elephant's trunk has
no bones? It contains about 40,000 muscles.

Did you know that what everyone thinks are flamingos' knees are actually their ankles? Flamingos stand on the tips of their toes, and their knees are actually much higher up, under their feathers.

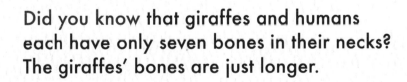

Did you know the blue whale has the largest bones of any living animal on land or water? Did you know that sharks don't have ANY bones?

Did you know that giraffes and humans each have only seven bones in their necks? The giraffes' bones are just longer.

Did you know that babies start out with around 270 bones? As humans grow, their bones fuse together. Adults typically have 206 bones.